8/'11
Leverett Library
75 Montague Road
Leverett,
Massachusetts 01054
413-548-9220
DISCARDED

Walrus

Tusk, Tusk

by Stephen Person

Walrus Consultant: Tony Fischbach, Wildlife Biologist
Walrus Research Program, Alaska Science Center, USGS
Anchorage, Alaska

Arctic Consultant: Dr. Steven C. Amstrup
Polar Bears International
www.polarbearsinternational.org

New York, New York

Credits

Cover and Title Page, © Steven Kazlowski/Science Faction/SuperStock; TOC, © Michael Kempf/iStockphoto; 4, © Steven Kazlowski/NGS Images; 5, © Brendan Smith/Wildlife Research Images; 6, © AP Images/U.S. Geological Survey/Steven Kazlowski; 8, © All Canada Photos/SuperStock; 9, © Kelvin Aitken/age fotostock/SuperStock; 10, © Paul Souders/Corbis; 11, © Göran Ehlmé; 12T, © W. Perry Conway/Corbis; 12B, © Robert Holmes/Corbis; 13, © Exactostock/SuperStock; 14, © Science Faction/SuperStock; 15, © Patrick Frischknecht/Still Pictures/Photolibrary; 16, © Paul Nicklen/National Geographic/Getty Images; 17, © Daniel J. Cox/Natural Exposures; 18, © Mary Evans Picture Library/Alamy; 19T, © J. Stephen Conn; 19B, © Accent Alaska/Alamy; 20, © Steven J. Kazlowski/NGS Images; 21, © Paul Souders/Corbis; 22, © age fotostock/SuperStock; 23, © All Canada Photos/SuperStock; 24–25, © AP Images/National Oceanic and Atmospheric Administration/Gary Friedrichsen; 25, © AP Images/U.S. Geological Survey/Tony Fischbach; 26, © AP Images/Woods Hole Oceanographic Institution/Carin Ashjian; 27, © Rinie Van Meurs/Foto Natura/Minden Pictures/Getty Images; 28, © Daniel J. Cox/Natural Exposures; 29T, © Martin Ruegner/Photolibrary; 29B, © All Canada Photos/SuperStock; 31, © Gail Johnson/Shutterstock; 32, © Antoine Beyeler/Shutterstock.

Publisher: Kenn Goin
Editorial Director: Adam Siegel
Creative Director: Spencer Brinker
Photo Researcher: Picture Perfect Professionals, LLC

Library of Congress Cataloging-in-Publication Data

Person, Stephen.
Walrus : tusk, tusk / by Stephen Person.
p. cm. — (Built for cold—arctic animals)
Includes bibliographical references and index.
ISBN-13: 978-1-61772-133-5 (library binding)
ISBN-10: 1-61772-133-6 (library binding)
1. Walrus—Juvenile literature. I. Title.
QL737.P62P46 2011
599.79'9—dc22

2010036463

For more information, write to Bearport Publishing Company, Inc., 101 Fifth Avenue, Suite 6R, New York, New York 10003. Printed in the United States of America in North Mankato, Minnesota.

121510
10810CGB

10 9 8 7 6 5 4 3 2 1

Contents

Adventures of a Biologist

The time is late spring, 2010. The place is the Chukchi (CHUK-chee) Sea, off the northwest **coast** of Alaska. **Wildlife biologist** Tony Fischbach has come here to study walruses—but no one said it would be easy.

Tony has to be very careful when he studies walruses. He knows that if the huge animals see, smell, or hear a human nearby, they will dive into the water.

Tony lies flat on his belly on a piece of floating sea ice. About 150 feet (46 m) ahead lie 20 sleeping walruses. Tony crawls closer to the giant animals, silently sliding a **crossbow** in front of him. In his teeth is an arrow. Attached to the arrow is a tiny **radio transmitter**. When Tony gets within 30 feet (9 m) of the walruses, he puts the arrow in the bow and takes careful aim.

Biologists in the Arctic sometimes wear white to blend in with the snow and ice. This helps them sneak up on walruses.

Hard Animals to Study

Tony fires his arrow. It sticks in the thick skin of a walrus. “It hardly bothers her,” Tony says. “She just lifts her head and turns to the walrus next to her with a look that says ‘What’s up?’ Then she goes back to sleep.” The radio transmitter will send information to Tony’s computer about where the walrus moves in the weeks ahead.

"Walruses are hard animals to study, because their **habitat** is so **remote**," Tony explains. They live only in the **Arctic region**, the northernmost place on Earth. They spend most of their lives swimming in icy ocean waters or resting on floating pieces of sea ice, called ice floes.

Walruses in the Wild

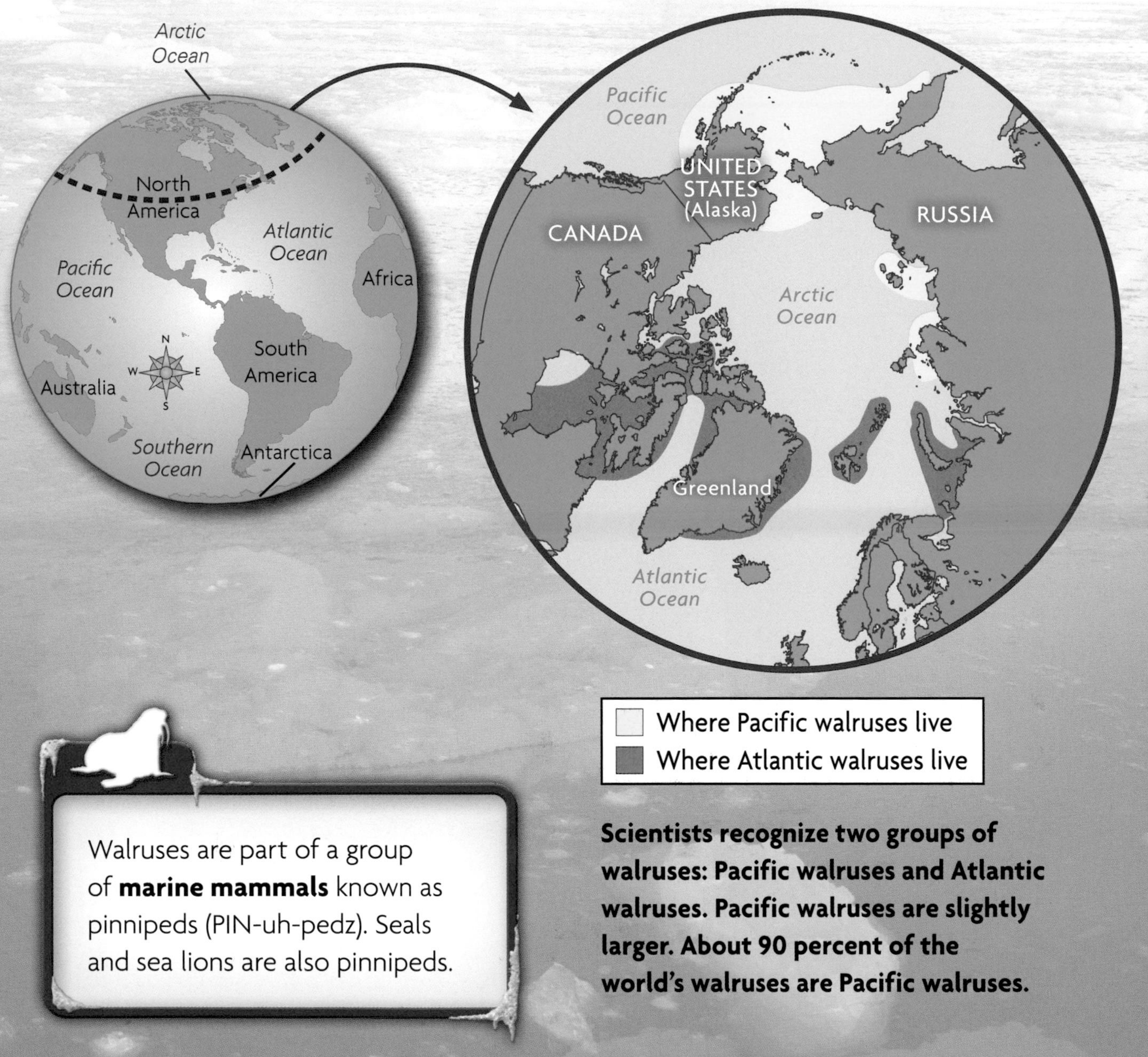

Scientists recognize two groups of walruses: Pacific walruses and Atlantic walruses. Pacific walruses are slightly larger. About 90 percent of the world's walruses are Pacific walruses.

Walruses are part of a group of **marine mammals** known as pinnipeds (PIN-uh-pedz). Seals and sea lions are also pinnipeds.

Built for the Arctic

There's another reason walruses are tough to study. The Arctic has one of the coldest **climates** on Earth. Walruses are usually found in temperatures from about 5°F to −40°F (−15°C to −40°C). "When I'm working out there, I have to put on layers of clothing to stay warm," Tony says. "The walruses, however, are laying out in the sun, feeling great!"

Like all other mammals, walruses cannot breathe underwater. Instead, they must come to the surface to get air.

Walruses can live comfortably in the Arctic because they are **adapted** for life in the cold. Beneath their skin is a layer of fat, called blubber, that can be up to four inches (10 cm) thick. Just like a winter coat, the blubber is very good **insulation**. It keeps the walrus's body heat inside the animal, allowing the walrus to stay warm in the bitter cold.

A thick layer of blubber keeps these walruses warm.

Whiskers at Work

The whiskers on a walrus also help the animal survive in the Arctic. A walrus has up to 700 whiskers on its **snout**. When a walrus is ready to feed, it dives to the bottom of the ocean. Swimming slowly, the walrus sweeps its whiskers along the soft sea floor. The whiskers feel for a walrus's favorite food: clams.

Beneath the walrus's whiskers are nerves that send information from the whiskers to the walrus's brain.

When the whiskers touch a clam, the walrus digs it up by spitting out jets of water. The walrus then takes the clam into its powerful mouth, sucks out the soft body, and spits out the shell. Walruses will eat up to 6,000 clams in one meal! “They dive to the bottom and spend about six minutes feeding,” Tony says. “Then they come up to breathe for a minute, and do it all over again.” Walruses usually **forage** like this for one or two days without rest—though some forage for up to seven days.

Walruses stir up clouds of sand as they feel for food on the sea floor.

Walruses spend most of their time in water that is less than 262 feet (80 m) deep. This is because clams are not usually found in deeper waters.

Join the Herd

Walruses spend about 80 percent of their lives in the water. When they're ready for a rest from swimming, they "haul out," or pull themselves up onto sea ice. "They're very **social** animals and like to haul out in large groups," Tony says. The walruses **communicate** by touching each other with their flippers and making barking and grunting sounds. "They really seem to know each other," says Tony.

In the water, walruses use their flippers to swim up to 20 miles per hour (32 kph). On ice or land they use them for walking—very slowly.

flippers

When there is no sea ice around, walruses will haul out onto islands or remote beaches.

In the summer, male and female walruses form separate **herds** when they haul out. Young walruses, called calves, haul out with their mothers. Tony often sees calves resting on their mothers' backs. "It's pretty funny," he says. "The females are tired from days of foraging. But the calves are fooling around, barking—they're full of energy!"

Walruses like to crowd together after they haul out because it helps keep them warm.

Battle of the Bulls

Haul-out spots are not all fun and games, though. "These places can be pretty **brutal**," Tony says. Using their **tusks** as weapons, walruses often poke at each other to protect their resting spaces. "You almost always find blood on the ice at haul-out spots," Tony explains.

Tusks are very long teeth that grow from the walrus's upper jaw. Male tusks can grow to be up to 39 inches (99 cm) long. Female tusks can grow up to 31 inches (79 cm).

Life for adult males, which are called bulls, can turn deadly in winter. Between the months of December and March, male and female herds come together to **mate**. First, however, bulls **compete** for the right to mate. They stab each other with their tusks, sometimes causing painful wounds. The strongest bulls are most likely to be chosen by females as mating partners.

Males are not usually big enough to fight for the right to mate until they are about 15 years old.

Walrus skin can be more than one inch (2.5 cm) thick. The thickest skin covers adult males on their necks and shoulders—where they are most likely to be stabbed by other walruses' tusks.

The Strongest Bond

About 15 months after mating, females haul out onto the sea ice to give birth. Walrus calves are born big—about four feet (1.2 m) long, and weighing from 100 to 150 pounds (45 to 68 kg). By the time they are one month old, the calves are already strong swimmers.

At haul-out spots, calves often sit on their mothers' backs. This helps keep them out of the reach of animals that want to eat them. It also protects the calves from being crushed by other walruses.

The bond between mothers and their young is very strong with walruses. Until a calf is at least two years old, it will spend almost every moment with its mother.

Like all other mammals, walruses drink their mothers' milk when they are young. Walrus mothers often **nurse** their calves while swimming. Mothers also teach the calves how to find food on the ocean floor. A calf will begin foraging for itself around its first birthday. Until that time, it has lived entirely on its mother's milk.

Mothers watch out for **predators**, such as polar bears and killer whales, that will eat calves. A mother will use her tusks to fight off these fierce animals.

A polar bear eating a baby walrus

Walruses and People

Polar bears and killer whales are threats to walruses, but they are not nearly as dangerous as human hunters. In the 1800s and early 1900s, hunters killed hundreds of thousands of walruses. So many walruses were killed that the animals nearly became **extinct**. Starting in the 1930s, countries with walruses made laws limiting walrus hunting. Now it is illegal for most people to kill walruses.

Walruses were valuable to hunters in the 1800s and 1900s because their blubber could be sold and melted into oil to burn in lamps.

Native peoples in the Arctic, however, are allowed to continue hunting walruses. Walrus hunting has been an important part of their **culture** for thousands of years. They use the meat and blubber for food and carve the tusks into jewelry and sculptures. They use the skin to cover the bottoms of boats. Native communities and wildlife managers work together to try to make sure that hunting does not threaten the walrus **population**.

Walrus-skin boats are made by stretching walrus skin over a wooden frame.

These sculptures were made from walrus tusks.

The total population of walruses today is about 250,000.

Follow the Ice

Each spring, walruses face a big challenge—a long **migration** north. Why do they make such a big journey from one part of the Arctic to another? They need to stay near the floating pieces of ice that cover shallow areas of the ocean. Doing so allows walruses to dive into the water, forage for clams, and then haul out onto the ice for a rest.

Walruses resting on sea ice

Walruses often migrate more than 1,800 miles (2,897 km) each year. They swim most of the way, but they also haul out onto floating ice and **drift** with the **current**.

The sea ice in the Arctic, however, doesn't always cover the same part of the ocean. It gets bigger and smaller depending on the time of the year. Sea ice covers the largest part of the ocean during the winter. In the spring, the sea ice in shallow areas of the southern Arctic begins melting. As a result, walruses head north to the Chukchi Sea, where the sea ice is still frozen. Unfortunately, in recent years the sea ice has been melting there as well.

Pacific Walrus Migration

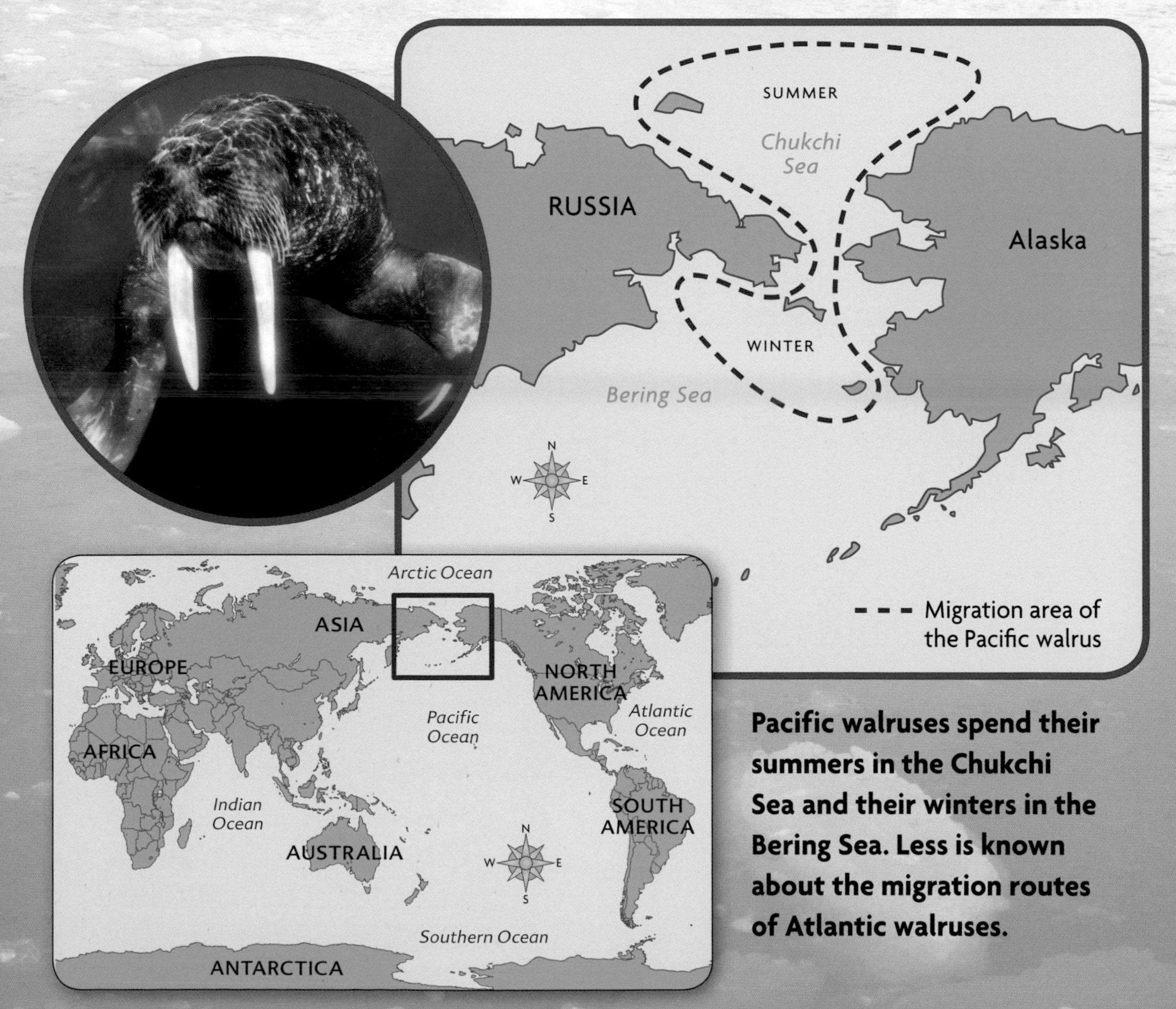

Pacific walruses spend their summers in the Chukchi Sea and their winters in the Bering Sea. Less is known about the migration routes of Atlantic walruses.

Dangers of Melting Ice

Why is there less sea ice in the Arctic than there was in the past? The answer is **global warming**. Temperatures around the world have been rising in the past 20 years, and they have been rising fastest in the Arctic. It is about 1.8 degrees Fahrenheit (1 degree Celsius) warmer in the Arctic than it was just 20 years ago. A warmer Arctic means less sea ice—and that's bad news for walruses.

Most climate scientists agree that global warming is caused by the burning of **fossil fuels**, such as coal and oil. When these fuels are burned, gases such as carbon dioxide are released. These gases trap the sun's heat near Earth, causing the planet to warm.

Power plants and car and truck engines produce most of the carbon dioxide emissions in many parts of the world.

In recent summers, ice has melted over shallow areas of the Chukchi Sea. Walruses still have to forage in this area, however, since this is where the clams live. They can't haul out there, though, since there is no ice to rest on. Instead, walruses must swim all the way to land. They crowd onto beaches in large herds, which can quickly lead to disaster.

In many parts of the Arctic, sea ice is forming a month later each fall than it did 20 years ago. It is melting three weeks earlier each spring.

Tragedy on the Beach

It is very dangerous for huge herds of walruses to crowd together on land. The sight of a polar bear, or even a loud noise, can cause the walruses to **panic**. When this happens, they race for the water, and calves can be crushed to death by adults. This is what most likely happened in September 2009.

These walruses crowded together on a haul-out spot in Alaska in 2009.

Scientists were flying over the northwest coast of Alaska when they spotted something terrible on the beach below. Nearly 150 walrus calves lay dead on the sand. The loss of sea ice is most likely to blame for these deaths. If temperatures had been cooler and ice had remained over the ocean as it used to, the calves would have been at sea instead of on land—and much safer.

"It was disturbing," Tony said after inspecting the dead calves. "They appeared to have been healthy."

Walruses can live up to 40 years.

Will Walruses Survive?

If Arctic ice continues melting, walruses will face a difficult challenge. Tony is especially worried about mothers and calves. As sea ice melts, mothers and their young are forced to make long swims to haul-out areas. They can get separated in the water or lost in stormy seas.

This walrus calf got separated from its mother in the ocean.

Scientists suspect that the walrus population has begun falling as a result of less Arctic sea ice. They predict that the sea ice will continue to shrink in the years ahead as a result of global warming.

"Mothers and young are the key to the walrus's future," Tony says. Walruses give birth just once every three years. As a result, when young walruses die, mothers can't replace them quickly. Will these animals be able to survive in a changing Arctic? Humans will help answer this question. If people can reduce global warming, then walruses will find the ice they need to **thrive** in their Arctic home.

Walrus mothers usually give birth to one calf at a time. Twins are very rare.

Walrus Facts

Walruses are social animals that like to crowd together when they haul out. Mothers with young calves form their own herds, which scientists call "nursery herds." Here are some more facts about these Arctic giants.

Weight	male adults usually weigh about 3,000 pounds (1,361 kg); female adults weigh about 2,000 pounds (907 kg)
Length	males grow up to 12 feet (4 m); females grow up to 9 feet (3 m)
Food	mainly clams, also crabs, mussels, sea worms, and large snails called welks; walruses will also eat seals
Life Span	up to 40 years
Habitat	Arctic region
Population	about 250,000

More Arctic Animals

The walrus is perfectly adapted for life in the sea and on the ice of the Arctic. Here are two more big marine mammals that make their homes in the Arctic region.

Killer Whale

- Killer whales are the largest members of the dolphin family. They grow to be up to 32 feet (10 m) long and weigh up to 22,000 pounds (9,979 kg).
- They will eat walruses, but they usually feed on seals, sea lions, fish, and seabirds.
- Killer whales hunt in groups, or pods, of up to 40 whales.
- Members of a pod communicate with each other by making sounds.
- Killer whales can swim up to 30 miles per hour (48 kph), making them one of the fastest marine mammals.
- They can live up to 80 years.

Bearded Seal

- Bearded seals are the largest seals in the Arctic. They can grow to be up to 8 feet (2.4 m) long and can weigh up to 800 pounds (363 kg).
- They are called "bearded" because of the long whiskers growing on their snouts.
- Like walruses, bearded seals use their whiskers to feel for clams and other food on the ocean floor.
- Unlike walruses, they are solitary animals, so they usually live alone.
- Bearded seals live about 25 years.

Glossary

adapted (uh-DAP-tid) changed over time to survive in an environment

Arctic region (ARK-tic REE-juhn) the northernmost area on Earth; it includes the Arctic Ocean, the North Pole, and northern parts of Europe, Asia, and North America, and is one of the coldest areas in the world

brutal (BROO-tuhl) extremely tough or difficult

climates (KLYE-mits) patterns of weather over a long period of time

coast (KOHST) land that runs along an ocean

communicate (kuh-MYOO-nuh-kayt) to share information, ideas, feelings, and thoughts

compete (kuhm-PEET) to struggle against others to gain something

crossbow (KROSS-*boh*) a powerful weapon used to fire arrows, often used for hunting

culture (KUHL-chur) the ideas, customs, and way of life of a group of people

current (KUR-uhnt) the movement of water in an ocean or river

drift (DRIFT) to be carried along by water or wind

extinct (ek-STINGKT) when a type of animal or plant completely dies out

forage (FOR-ij) to look for food in the wild

fossil fuels (FOSS-uhl FYOO-uhlz) energy sources made from the remains of plants and animals that died millions of years ago, such as coal, oil, and gas

global warming (GLOHB-uhl WORM-ing) the gradual warming of Earth's air and oceans caused by a buildup of greenhouse gases, which trap heat from the sun in Earth's atmosphere

habitat (HAB-uh-*tat*) the place in the wild where an animal or a plant normally lives

herds (HURDS) large groups of animals

insulation (*in*-suh-LAY-shuhn) something that prevents heat from escaping

marine mammals (muh-REEN MAM-uhlz) warm-blooded animals that live in the ocean, have hair or fur on their skin, and drink their mothers' milk as babies

mate (MAYT) to come together to produce young

migration (mye-GRAY-shuhn) a journey from one place to another at a certain time of the year

native (NAY-tiv) belonging to a particular place because of where one was born

nurse (NURSS) to feed a young animal milk that comes from its mother

panic (PAN-ik) to feel a sudden fright or terror

population (*pop*-yuh-LAY-shuhn) the total number of a kind of animal living in a place

predators (PRED-uh-turz) animals that hunt other animals for food

radio transmitter (RAY-dee-oh tranz-MIT-ur) an object that sends out radio signals and is put on an animal so that its movements can be tracked

remote (ri-MOHT) far from any settled place

snout (SNOUT) the long front part of an animal's head that sticks out; it includes the nose and usually the jaws and mouth as well

social (SOH-shuhl) living in groups and enjoying contact with others

thrive (THRIVE) to grow or to do well

tusks (TUHSKS) long, pointed teeth, such as those on an elephant or a walrus

wildlife biologist (WILDE-life bye-OL-uh-jist) a scientist who studies wild animals living in their natural environment

Bibliography

Alaska Department of Fish & Game ("Walrus: Wildlife Notebook Series") (www.adfg.state.ak.us/pubs/notebook/marine/walrus.php)

Sea World ("Walrus") (www.seaworld.org/animal-info/info-books/walrus/index.htm)

U.S. Fish & Wildlife Service/Marine Mammals Management ("About Walrus") (alaska.fws.gov/fisheries/mmm/walrus/nhistory.htm)

Read More

Knudtson, Peter. *The World of the Walrus.* San Francisco: Sierra Club Books for Children (1998).

Miller, Sara Swan. *Walruses of the Arctic (Brrr! Polar Animals).* New York: PowerKids Press (2009).

Orme, Helen. *Climate Change (Earth in Danger).* New York: Bearport (2009).

Rotter, Charles. *Walruses.* Chanhassen, MN: Child's World (2001).

Learn More Online

To learn more about walruses, visit
www.bearportpublishing.com/BuiltforCold

Index

About the Author

Stephen Person has written many children's books about history, science, and the environment. He lives with his family in Saratoga Springs, New York.